THINGS I WANTED
MY GRANDSON TO KNOW
before I leave

THINGS I WANTED MY GRANDSON TO KNOW

before I leave

KENN STOBBE

iUniverse LLC
Bloomington

THINGS I WANTED MY GRANDSON TO KNOW BEFORE I LEAVE

iUniverse books may be ordered through booksellers or by contacting:

iUniverse LLC
1663 Liberty Drive
Bloomington, IN 47403
www.iuniverse.com
1-800-Authors (1-800-288-4677)

Because of the dynamic nature of the Internet, any web addresses or links contained in this book may have changed since publication and may no longer be valid. The views expressed in this work are solely those of the author and do not necessarily reflect the views of the publisher, and the publisher hereby disclaims any responsibility for them.

Any people depicted in stock imagery provided by Thinkstock are models, and such images are being used for illustrative purposes only. Certain stock imagery © Thinkstock.

ISBN: 978-1-4917-2733-1 (sc)
ISBN: 978-1-4917-2732-4 (e)

Library of Congress Control Number: 2014904576

Printed in the United States of America.

iUniverse rev. date: 04/01/2014

Cover Photography and Consulting
Lindsy Gumb
LG Photography
Lindsygumbphotography.com
Burwell Nebraska

Special Thanks:
To my God for giving me the courage to
speak from my heart and letting me live
in the beautiful Nebraska Sandhills

In memory of
"Missy"
(Kathleen Miles)
1947-2014
Big as the Sky!

Introduction

My dearest Grayson,

I was already an old man when you were born so chances of me being around to tell you these things while you are growing up are pretty slim. From the day you were born I began making a list of old sayings, quotations, snippets, lessons I've learned, beliefs, and observations that I believe helped make me who I am; some I read, others were told to me by friends and loved ones, and still others were my own thoughts. Many made me laugh, and many brought tears to my eyes, but all made me think. I thought all were worth knowing and remembering. You are the son I never had and my aim is to share them with you in hopes they might make you a better person, and your journey through this life just a little easier. Only you, your loved ones and friends will ever know if I hit my mark.

There is a God, one God, and His love for us is unconditional and never ending.

Horses probably buck because they don't like people sittin' on 'em.

Always drink from the creek upstream from the herd.

Not everything on the ground in the corral is dirt.

God made mosquitoes, flies, and sandburs to remind us that we are sinners.

Never try to count your blessings 'cause you'll never be able to count that high. And besides, sometimes you will get a blessing and not even know it.

You can never go wrong with Butter Pecan ice cream.

Grandma doesn't really think the firemen will care if your underwear is clean.

Always try and think before you speak, words can hurt and that hurt lasts far longer than a punch in the nose.

I think bulls spend their entire life in a bad mood.

Choose your words carefully; someday you may have to eat them.

It's far better to let people think you're a fool then to open your mouth and remove all doubt.

BIBLE stands for Basic Instructions Before Leaving Earth.

Sometimes it doesn't matter what you say, but it always matters how you say it.

Crayon marks on the wall will wash off.

When you hurt somebody, it's like driving a nail into a piece of wood, you can remove the nail, but the hole will always be there.

It's okay for men to cry, grandpa does his share.

Tears of joy are far better than tears of sorrow.

Good or bad, like it or not, your heart has a mind all its own. You can tell it what to do but it won't listen at all.

Your heart is big enough to love more than one.

"Love" is probably the most overused word in the entire world.

Human nature makes us always want to be first, but being best is a whole lot better.

Remember, it's hard to start a fire with wet wood.

Never try and drown your sorrows, I learned a long time ago they know how to swim.

Don't put the key to your happiness in someone else's pocket; keep it in your own.

Loving your grandma and loving Butter Pecan Ice Cream are not the same.

Worry is like riding a rocking horse; it passes the time, but doesn't take you anywhere.

Anger serves no useful purpose.

Being a cowboy isn't a state of mind, it's a way of life.

If something doesn't look like it's worth the effort, it probably isn't.

Sometimes being silent may be your best answer.

Arguments and fights only prove who's louder or stronger, not who's right or wrong. Sometimes it's real hard, but always try and avoid both.

Walking away from a fight does not mean you're a coward. But if a fight is absolutely unavoidable, don't throw the first punch but do your darnedest to throw the last.

When it comes to horses, admire the big one, but saddle the small one.

Be willing to defend those who can't defend themselves.

It's hard to put your foot in your mouth if it's shut.

If you sleep 8 hours every day, you will have missed 1/3 of your entire life.

We are not born with real contentment, we must learn it.

I guess it's always better to be a "has been" than a "never was".

The hardest thing you will have to do in life is love your neighbor as yourself.

If you always speak kind words, nobody will resent them.

Big or small, all blessings come from God, and like you, He likes to hear "Thank You" now and then too.

It is far better to make dust than to eat dust.

There is a big difference between friends and acquaintances, acquaintances will come and go but true friends last forever.

It's okay to remember past loves, they've helped make you who you are.

Always remember your word is your honor.

Giving credit where credit is due ain't always easy, but it's the right thing to do.

Try and remember your bad decisions, they make for great stories around the campfire.

Never go into anything if you don't know the way out.

All blessings are really presents from God but He doesn't wrap them in shiny paper and ribbons, so sometimes they're hard to recognize.

Don't make promises you know you will have a hard time keepin'.

Good morals and good values are worth far more and will last far longer than money and a new pick-up.

A good friend is someone who laughs at your jokes even when they're not funny.

Be forthright and honest is all your business dealings, your handshake is your bond.

There's only two things you'll find on the back of a bull, fools and flies.

Your life will be a lot more enjoyable if you choose friends that share your morals and values. Your church is a great place to find 'em.

It's perfectly fine to say you made a mistake and even better if you learn from it. Take notice of the mistakes others make and learn from them too.

Practice saying "I'm sorry" you will say it often during your life time.

Finishing last is far better than not finishing at all.

It's one thing to know the right thing to do, the hard part is doin' it.

A sure sign of manhood is admitting when you are wrong.

Never, ever tell your girlfriend or wife that her new teeth braces look like the grill of your pick-up. Never!

When you're far away, aim high and remember the wind.

I believe you can tell a lot about the character of a man by his handshake, always extend your hand and grip firmly, it communicates confidence.

Remember, once you are over the hill, you pick up speed.

Don't squat with your spurs on.

Your cowboy boots will get a lot tougher to get on and off, the older you get.

Always be cautious of people who make promises you know they can't keep. This includes most politicians.

It's very difficult, if not impossible, to fill another man's boots. Be content with who you are and always be yourself.

Always be willing to lend a helping hand. And never be too proud to ask for one.

Be willing to work hard for the things you want. You will appreciate them that much more. A little prayer never hurts either.

Read the Bible a little bit every single day, you will be a better man for it.

Time spent on your knees in prayer is priceless.

Slaps in the face sting like heck, so don't say or do anything to a woman that might get you one.

Beautiful sunrises and sunsets are a lot more beautiful when you share them with someone you love.

It should be quite evident why God gave you two ears and only one mouth.

The biggest trouble maker in your life will be the guy who watches you shave and brush your teeth in the mirror every morning.

Never ask others for forgiveness until you can forgive others.

Sorrow and heartache is like carrying a big rock, the longer you carry it the heavier it gets.

Live a good, honorable life, and when you're my age and think back, you can enjoy it a second time.

Don't judge a book or a person by their cover. It's what's inside that counts.

Never be afraid to try.

Learn to say, "Thanks, Honey, that's just the way I like it", even when the yolks are hard and the biscuits burnt.

Impress people by the way you live your life, not by the things you can buy.

"Please" will get you a lot further down the road than "Give me".

Life is like a shadow on the ground, it changes by the second.

Your dog is the best example of a loyal friend that I can think of. You can tell it all your troubles, forget to feed it, leave it out in the weather, yell at it and call it names. It will always greet you with a wagging tail and loving lick. If you need proof, lock your wife or girlfriend in the trunk of your car along with your dog and see which one is happier to see you when you open it again.

Compliment people every chance you get, they like to hear it just as much as you.

You need clouds in your life before you can have silver linings.

The only people you need to get even with are the ones that helped you along the way.

There is nothing like the smell right after a rain or the sight of a rainbow. Stop whatever you're are doing and enjoy them. Then thank God for them.

Afternoon naps recharge your batteries, you'll need more recharging the older you get.

There is so much more to life than a series of 8 second rides with a shiny gold buckle waiting at the end. Life will buck you off more times than you can count, always pick yourself up, dust yourself off and get right back on again.

Don't ever expect life to be fair.

There are three kinds of people in this world. Those that make things happen, those that let things happen, and those poor souls that don't even have a suspicion. Try to be a leader, not a follower.

Don't ever smoke or chew or you'll burn holes in your favorite shirt or have slobber running down the side of your pick-up. Not cool!

Always be a gentleman and treat your gal with respect, open doors for her, and slide out her chairs. Give her a flower on special occasions. Yeah, your buddies will call you a wuss but your gal with think you're special.

Never raise your hand to a woman in anger.

Sins are sins, there's no such thing as big ones or little ones.

Be responsible, if you commit a crime; be prepared to do the time.

If you don't tell lies, you won't have to worry about remembering everything you said in the past.

Treat law enforcement officers with respect, they deserve it and besides, they have the unique ability to make your life miserable.

Thank God before eating his bounty at every meal.

Whenever you are introduced to a person, man or woman, extend your hand. It's a form of hospitality and welcome.

Use napkins to wipe your mouth, not to blow your nose, especially in the presence of women.

Alcohol on your breath hurts your credibility.

Drinking alcohol is not a right of passage and has absolutely no connection to manliness. Drink in moderation if you can handle it, and don't drink if you can't. It's that simple. Nothing good ever happens when you drink too much.

You can't be lost if you don't care where you are.

Once I opened a door for a liberated woman who immediately turned and asked me if I opened the door just because she was a woman? "No, ma'am", I said, "I opened the door for you just because I'm a gentleman, don't have a darn thing to do with what you are." Always try to be a gentleman, it's not that tough, and be proud of it. There's getting to be fewer and fewer of 'em.

As long as you are physically able, pray on your knees, it's a tangible way to show God respect.

If you don't know what it is, or what it does, don't mess with it.

When you are just about ready to "throw in the towel", remember that God never gives you more than you can handle. If God brings you to it, He will bring you through it.

Humility is a very worthy virtue and playing golf is the fastest way to learn it.

Too much alcohol always makes you think you're smarter than you really are.

Things can change, never tattoo a woman's name on your body, your horse's or dog's name is a better choice.

I know your grandma says that eating bacon and butter will kill you, and she just might be right. But I've been hearing that now for over 37 years, so it must be an awful slow death.

Someday when you have children of your own, they will break your rules, don't over react. Make the punishment fit the crime. I can't count the number of times I grounded your mother for life, never once thinking that I'd be gone long before her. So how would I ever know if she obeyed?

Always address your gal's folks as "sir" and "ma'am" unless invited to do otherwise.

Most any male can be a sperm donor, not near as many can be a good father.

Kids might not be planned but they are never mistakes. God never makes mistakes.

Only God knows if caterpillars and box turtles ever get where they're going.

Never carry your gun with a bullet in the chamber.

As long as grandma and I have been together, I have always helped her clear the table and do the dishes, do the same for your gal.

Respect and trust are not presents to be handed out, they both must be earned, and once either is lost, they are hard to get back, if ever.

By and large, Democrats are good people who pretty much want the same things you do; they just go about gettin' it the wrong way.

Liberals are really just very angry Democrats. Their ideas will always cost you freedoms or money. Avoid them like you would an angry skunk.

Always wear your jeans up around your waist and wear your ball cap with the bill facing forward. At least people will think you know if you're coming or going, even if you really don't.

Learn to cook and how to wash clothes, there might not always be someone around to do it for you.

Yes, ducks, geese, and cranes do get tired from flying all day. That's why they stop to rest all night.

Sometimes a simple roll of toilet paper can be a prized possession. Always know where to get one in a hurry and remember what I said about squatting with your spurs on.

It's okay to be scared or afraid, they make you cautious.

Bluebirds, orioles, and yellow finches are living proof that God thought of everything.

An old friend told me once that only pirates pierce their ears, so if you ever come home with pierced ears, there better be a ship out in the front yard.

Your dad, your grandpas and someday your sons and grandsons are the only men you should ever kiss, ever.

Tell people that you love them often, there will come a day when you wish you could.

When you close your eyes and think of simple pleasures, Oreo cookies soaked in ice cold milk will always make the cut.

Fish fight 'cause they don't want to get in the boat, really.

If you want to put a smile on a young ladies' face, kiss the back of her hand.

Call your banker by his first name, greet him with a handshake and always ask about his family. It will make your business with him a lot easier.

I know your mom and your grandma think they know most everything. No harm, just let 'em keep on thinkin' it.

I used to tell my friends that if there was ever anything they couldn't figure out on their own, to call your mom, 'cause she had all the answers. That really made her angry and I think hurt a little, I should have known better.

Thank God that your mom and grandma don't charge a fee for their advice. The bill would resemble the national debt.

Never go to bed angry.

I learned years ago that there is a direct relationship between big mouths and small brains.

It's hard to respect others without first respecting yourself.

Everybody, and I mean everybody, sins, makes mistakes, and errors in judgment, so don't get down on yourself if you do. There was only one perfect being, His name was Jesus Christ.

There is a big difference between "self-esteem" and "self-respect". Self-esteem is liking yourself for what you can do; self-respect is liking yourself for who you are. Learn to tell the difference, and if you have to choose between the two, take self-respect.

If you absolutely have to pick your nose or your seat, do it in private.

Live simply, try to avoid borrowing money, but if you must, don't borrow more than you can comfortably pay back and pay it back as quickly as you can.

It's far better to be a good listener than a talking head.

I often ask others for their perspective about subjects that trouble me. If you do, respect their opinion, especially since you asked for it; but keep in mind that opinions are like noses and butts, most everybody will have one.

Try your best to be a good listener, look people directly in the eyes when they speak and don't interrupt.

Until you are lucky enough to be your own boss, do what your boss tells you, even when you don't agree.

It is always more comforting when someone else wipes away your tears of sorrow.

You can have many loves in your lifetime, but only one mom. Never lose sight of that, and always treat her like someone very special, 'cause she is.

Always mend fences with your friends and neighbors even if you weren't the one who cut 'em.

You can only reap what you sow. Sow good things like love, patience, understanding, forgiveness, humility and your harvest will always be bountiful.

You can always learn a lot from watching livestock and wildlife. Learn to trust your instincts. If it looks like a duck, swims like a duck, quacks like a duck; chances are pretty darn good that it's a duck.

Try not to stare at a woman's body parts, but for those times when you just can't help yourself, be wearing your sun glasses.

There's a real knack to knowing which cow pies you can kick and which ones you can't, until you learn it, it's best to just step over 'em or go around 'em, especially on a hot day.

The wind usually blows out here so always head into the wind when you're stalking game, and never spit into it.

There are some people who will never hear a Bobwhite whistle, a coyote howl, or see an eagle soar, that's a shame.

Republicans are not always right, and Democrats not always wrong, just mostly.

Think twice before wearing a bow tie with a cowboy shirt.

If you're riding on a high horse, there's no way to get down gracefully.

Never wipe your nose or your mouth in the sleeve of your shirt unless it's an emergency, and never at the supper table, no matter what.

The art of riding a horse is keeping the horse between you and the ground.

Girls seem to like a man who can dance, if you want to meet a lot of young ladies, learn to dance. You don't have to like it, just do it.

If you don't know where you're goin', it's probably a good idea not to use your spurs.

Several of my friends say that I look like a wounded Rhinoceros when I dance, but, I wonder how many of them have ever seen a wounded Rhino two step?

You don't have to kneel and pray every time you want to talk to God. It's really no different than talking to me or your dad. God is always there and always listening.

A cowboy is one who says that it was nothin' when it was everything.

Always keep a healthy supply of dog treats in your pick-up. It will make the journey to your neighbor's front door a lot easier.

Never leave home without your pocket cross and rub it often to remind yourself that God loves you.

When you lose, don't lose the lesson.

You weren't born with your hat on your head so know when to remove it, and don't worry; you are not the only person to get hat hair.

Have heard it said that the only good reason to ride a bull is to meet a pretty nurse.

Always get the manure off your boots and remove your hat went entering the Lord's house.

It's okay to stop and ask for directions, and especially well advised on the long journey of life.

In matters of love, never ask a question of a gal when the answer might break your heart unless you're prepared to deal with a broken heart.

Don't be afraid to go after what you want, or what you want to be. But always be willing to pay the price.

Be humble when saying you're sorry or asking for forgiveness. Holding your hat in your hand is a good start.

Never judge your gal by her relatives.

No one says "it's only a game" when their team is winning.

Pray for things that matter, God doesn't really care what you drive, so don't waste His time and yours praying for a new pick-up.

Bad things do happen to good people.

Always be yourself because the people that matter don't mind . . . and the ones that mind don't matter.

Life isn't tied with a bow . . . but it's still a gift.

Every new day is created by God, thank Him for it.

If you always help your neighbors brand their calves, you'll never be short handed when it's time to brand your own.

When choosing your life's work, keep in mind that not everybody would make a good doctor or lawyer, but not everybody would make a good ranch hand either.

There is no shame in working with your hands and your back for a living. Do your work heartily; it's the Lord for whom you really work.

A callused hand is usually a strong hand.

Bunions hurt like the devil, always wear boots that fit.

Few things are more relaxing than flying a kite or skipping rocks. Do them every chance you get, especially with your kids.

Once a long time ago, while having a little disagreement with your grandma, I told her that I'd like to agree with her, but if I did, then we'd both be wrong. I've never said it since. It's okay to think it, just don't ever say it.

Sometimes during your life you will lose your perspective, women seem to have a real talent for getting it back for you.

If you read the Bible and worship regularly, you will hear the words "mercy" and "grace" often. Think about them like this. "Mercy" is not getting punished even though you deserve to. "Grace" is getting something nice even though you don't deserve to.

Always try and sleep where you can see the stars, somehow they magically help you forget the troubles of the day.

Sometimes I wish the little voice inside me would just be silent.

Some people say that there are no do-overs in real life, they're mistaken, for Christians every new day is a mulligan.

Big cities are a good place to go a few times a year to visit friends or stock up on supplies. They're not a good place to spend your life or raise your kids.

I guess I don't really know and surely couldn't explain why my eyes well up with tears when I hear the Star Spangled Banner; but I'm not ashamed of it.

Whenever a funeral procession crosses your path, lower your head and ask the Lord to comfort the family and loved ones left behind. It's too late to pray for the person in the coffin.

Whenever you're in grandma's presence, cheer for the Green Bay Packers, and never, ever switch channels when she's watchin' them on TV.

The two most beautiful prayers ever sung are *God Bless America* and *The Lord's Prayer.*

I don't know why Mourning Doves sound so sad and lonely, but they sure do.

Love is not a game; there are no winners or losers, just joys and sorrows.

Cursing and swearing is a bad habit to get into although I think most people have done it a time or two. Even grandma does it now and then, except she tries to do it under her breath so no one hears.

Never spend hard earned money for a cat. I'm sure God had more in mind for 'em than catching mice. I just don't know what that would be though.

A long line of smoke on the horizon usually means a prairie fire. Always grab a shovel and head that way. Those fighting the fire can always use an extra hand.

The saddest sounds I've ever heard are *Taps* blown by a distant bugler and a piper playing *Amazing Grace* on a bagpipe; they always send chills up my spine and put a lump in my throat.

People out here just take stars for granted; there are people who live in big cities that never see them, if they only knew what they were missing.

As many times as sheep and shepherds are referenced in the Bible, I've never understood why they always seem to get such a bad rap.

Always, always make your first jump into a strange lake feet first.

I have heard it said that silence is golden, don't know about that, but do know it's darn valuable.

All you can do is all you can do, just don't ever quit.

Turn to the Lord often out of gratitude and you won't be a stranger when you turn to him in desperation; and you will.

If you're the first one on the serving bowl, always leave enough to make it around the table at least once. And when there's only one portion left, ask if anyone wants to share.

Try and make your home where the seasons change, each season has its very own beauty. Just visit all those other places.

Plant lots of trees, their splendor as they change with the seasons will take your breath away.

You will probably live a lot longer than grandpa so take good care of your body. I wish I would have. They make replacement parts, and I have a few, but they never seem to work as well as your original equipment and they are darn expensive.

Set a goal for yourself that when the Lord calls you home, you leave no man or woman behind that is glad to see you go, I still have some work to do.

When a cook serves something you're not too fond of, never snub your nose. Take a small helping, leave it on your plate and claim you are too full to eat it. Men cooks won't care if you snub your nose, but some women cooks take it real personal.

If you think you want to be a rodeo cowboy, your mom and grandma would like you to take a long look at calf roping. Leave the bucking events to cowboys who don't think they will ever get old and have a lot of money for those replacement parts.

Remember you are never as tough as you think you are, or want to be.

Ask God early for a goodly share of patience, you'll need plenty.

When you are having words with a woman, more times than not, you won't get to use yours.

When you are my age, as hard as it might be to get down on the floor to play with your grandkids, do it anyway. The laughter and joy on their faces will reward your effort, and somebody will always help you get back up.

Being able to poke fun at yourself is a sure sign of self-confidence. It takes a good man not to poke fun at others.

While your children and grandkids are small, help them plant a tree the same size as they are and watch them grow together. Someday when you're gone, they will look at that tree and think of you.

I've heard it said that cowboys who ride bulls were probably not their class valedictorian.

Buy a camera and keep it close. Take lots of pictures of friends, loved ones, beautiful things and places, if you do, you won't have to try near as hard to remember the things you wish you could when you are my age.

God loves us far too much to make bad things happen, but he allows bad things to happen to teach us and do his will.

There's a big, big difference between growing older and growing up. Growing older is mandatory, growing up is optional.

Our Lord doesn't make deals, so don't waste your time by including "If You" closely followed by "I will" in any of your prayers or conversations with Him.

Never think of a cat as a pet. Keep a few around the place to keep rodents away, treat 'em as you would any of God's creatures, but never let 'em indoors. Think of 'em as a four legged hired hand.

I used to find it amusing how many men wore cowboy hats that probably never even walked past a horse, then grandma pointed out that most likely, a very large number of men who wear baseball caps never played baseball either. She's a smart woman.

God only promises a safe landing, not a calm passage.

Always seek good counsel when about to make an important decision. There's no better place to start than on your knees.

There was a period of time in my life that I thought I was really big and important. Then once while on vacation, I stood on the rim of the Grand Canyon, and it didn't take very long for me to realize how infinitesimal I really am.

Politely listen to advice given to you by others but always listen closest to the voice inside yourself.

I've heard it said that you can tell a lot about a man by the kind of pet he owns. When you decide to get a dog, give Labradors strong consideration. I've always found them to be big, strong, mostly silent, very loyal, obedient, easy going, gentle, good with kids, and great hunters and swimmers, heck, they are most everything I want to be.

It's true that a person can never have too many friends, and good friends are like angels, you don't have to see them to know they are there.

A good hunt is not measured by what's in your game bag or the size of the rack. Enjoy the sights, smells, sounds of creation, and the time spent with buddies. On some of my most memorable hunts, I never fired a single shot.

People my age usually don't have regrets for what we did, but rather for what we didn't do, and I have some.

Don't over-harvest the fish or game. Take what you need for a meal or two, thank God for the experience and leave the rest to help you create new memories.

Exercise your right to vote every time you're given the opportunity. Thousands of good men and women gave their lives so you have that right. Don't let their memories and sacrifices be in vain.

If you are ever wondering how you should vote, get your Bible and read Ecclesiastes 10:2. That verse should help you decide.

Always respect the American Flag and those brave men and women who defend it every day. If your country ever calls on you to defend it, do it with determination and honor.

Let your faith always be greater than your fear.

When your mother was young, every morning before sending her off to school I'd kiss the palm of her hand and tell her that if she ever needed a hug during the day to hold that palm up next to her cheek to remind her how much I loved her. Do the same, not just for your kids but all those you love. Often times I lay in bed at night regretting that I didn't kiss more palms. I find a lot of comfort in believing that the last thing God does before sending every new baby out into the world is kiss their palm.

Go out of your way to thank and show appreciation for any veteran or person still wearing the uniform of their country. And if you can, pick up their tab.

I have always been in awe of thunderstorms, and spend a lot time on stormy nights just sitting in the dark watching and listening. I believe thunder is the Lord's way of telling me, "We need to talk", and we do.

You will have to go to school when you are a young lad growing up; it's the law, so make the best of it. Pay attention and study hard, when you are my age you will be glad you did, although try as I might, I can never remember using algebra.

I believe that athletics not only make you a better student but also teach you skills that you can use your entire life. Not everybody can be the starting quarterback or pitcher, that's why they are called "team" sports. And I'd bet your gal will still think you are special even if you sit the pines.

Life is not a race that you run, but a long journey that you take, and it's mostly up hill and often into a head wind.

There is a huge difference between being a good sport and a good loser. A good sport is gracious and humble in both victory and defeat. A good loser is still a loser.

Laugh, laugh, and laugh even more. Laugh often, long and hard. Try to make others laugh too. Tears from laughter are much sweeter than tears from sorrow. Never laugh at others, only with them, and don't be afraid to laugh at yourself.

Don't be in a hurry to grow up. Play cowboys and Indians, cops and robbers, crawl on your hands and knees driving your toy trucks. You will grow up soon enough. Grandma still tells me to grow up from time to time, but I don't think I ever really want to, at least all the way.

Sing, make joyous noise every chance you get. Sing in church, in the shower, runnin' on down the highway in your pick-up and while you're working. Sing to your kids and even your gal or wife. Singing will keep your heart young. And many songs have a way of saying things that you think but can't put into words. Music is what feelings sound like.

They say "Absence makes the heart grow fonder", but I think absence with a broken heart only makes the heart grow heavier. And time does not heal all wounds, some wounds never heal, all you do is pick up the pieces and carry on as best you can.

When you are praying or just talking with the Lord, don't worry about finding the right words, He already knows what you want to say.

One of the hardest decisions you'll ever face in life is choosing whether to walk away, or try harder.

During your life you will probably have many romances, and you will believe that each one is "the" one, but more than likely, your heart will be broken a time or two. Reminisce and learn from each broken heart because they will help mold you into the man that some young lady will think is truly "the" one.

When you are down to your last round of ammunition, relax, take a deep breath, take careful aim and make it count.

Always be on the lookout for people who might be down on their luck and need a helping hand. Be willing to offer that helping hand any way you can, money, food, clothes, whatever it takes, 'cause everything you have was given to you as a blessing, everything!

Don't ever let the collection plate pass by you without giving the Lord His due. And don't think of your offering as just another bill that must be paid, it is a form of worship.

You will find that not all people share your beliefs, especially when it comes to faith and how you worship the Lord. It is important to respect the beliefs of others whether or not you agree with them.

We Christians observe Christmas and Easter, Jews observe Passover and Hanukah. Atheists observe April Fool's Day, and rightly so.

Some dates are real important to remember, loved one's birthdays rank up there pretty high. And unless you really enjoy sleepin' in your pick-up, don't ever forget your wedding anniversary.

Your gal or wife should never have to cook on three occasions, her birthday, Mother's Day, and your anniversary. On those special days, take her out to a nice restaurant instead, and a bottle of wine or flowers is also a nice touch.

"Pity" is an ugly word that implies you are better than another person. You can have compassion or sympathy for another, but never pity them. And as long as you know how to pray, you'll never have cause to pity yourself.

You make a living by what you get; you make a life by what you give.

There is a very fine line between pride and conceit, be careful not to cross it. Conceit changes a man, you might like what you see in the mirror but your friends won't like what they see when looking at you.

Sometimes it dawns on me that I don't understand everything I know.

Attend to your own business and let others mind theirs, don't gossip or listen to those who do. If you are not willing to say it to another's face, it's best not to say it, period.

Read a lot of good books. History books will teach you about your birthright, documentaries will enlighten you, political books will sometimes make you angry and the Bible will give you peace. Your mind will always stay sharp if you read.

Time can be so cruel, when you're in a hospital waiting room yearning for news, and you want it to fly, it passes oh so slowly: but when you're in the arms of your lover and never want the moment to end, it flies

"Bucket List" is a catchy term for a list of things you want to do before you die. You will have a lot of years to make your list. I have two bucket lists, one I can share with people, the other I can't. And for those old folks who don't have a bucket list, I can't help but wonder what motivates them to get out of bed every morning.

You'll often hear people my age say, "I don't know what I'd do with myself if I retired." Feel sorry for them.

If your girlfriend or wife ever tells you she wants to be treated like one of the guys, it might be a good indication that you're spending too much time with the guys.

I like to be on a first name basis with my physician, I would have difficulty allowing a stranger to do to me what he has to do.

I also like to call my pastor by his first name when we are out of the sanctuary. I'm sure several of my Christian friends find that irreverent, but it sure makes it easier for me to tell him what's troubling me.

Family traditions are a nice way of remembering those we love, those still with us and those who aren't. Your great grandma's sugar cookies at Christmas time is one tradition you should always keep.

The most beautiful and powerful hymn I've ever heard is "How Great Thou Art". When you hear it, close your eyes and just concentrate on the words.

I've wasted a lot of time looking, but have yet to find a suitable substitute for plain old common sense.

One of your grandma's sisters had a little retort when people would razz her a little. She'd ask," Was that kind, necessary and true?" Ask yourself that when what you are about to say might sting someone. And just for the record, that sister seldom practiced what she preached.

Golf is game I love to hate. I always swing at the ball real hard just in case I hit it. Your best round is just a few strokes shy of being your worst. And if you golf, don't confuse luck with skill.

Unless you're a slacker, never be afraid to ask others how they think you're doin'. But also be prepared for how they might answer.

Experience is a wonderful teacher, but the lessons are not always pleasant.

Independence can be very rewarding and satisfying, and very lonely too.

Getting old is a lot more fun than being old but a friend once told me that it's still the best alternative.

Guess I never fully understood what it meant to be "comfortable in my own skin". I always figured I was, but then again, I didn't know I had a choice. Don't talk in riddles.

Your mother was very independent when she was growing up; she stretched her wings and wanted to fly solo earlier than most. I don't think she ever anticipated all the crash landings though. She still carries a few scars as reminders. It's good to look at old scars and remember how we got them.

Real courage is knowing that what you are about to attempt is next to impossible, and you continue on anyway.

Life is too short, ride your best horse first.

Your mom often reminded me of an old shop radio I had, it was either blaring or giving me static and was harder than the dickens to get tuned in.

I was pretty strict with your mom, I was one of those "my way or the highway" dads. Don't be like I was. God, how I wish I could go back in time and raise her again.

When I go home, don't dwell on my death but rather my life and take all that love you have for me and spread it around.

Just because the trail you're followin' is well marked, doesn't mean the person who marked it knew where they were headed.

If you ever have the opportunity to speak in front of a group of people, shy away from using the word "I" very often.

If you don't know something, just own up, it's okay. But then turn around and try to learn what you didn't know.

Don't beat around the bush, always say what you mean and, more importantly, mean what you say.

It's fun to go out and have a few with the guys now and then, but know when to call it a night. You'll never soar with the eagles all day when you've been out hootin' with the owls all night.

Unfortunately, not only stupid people do stupid things, stupidity is an equal opportunity affliction.

It is true, what goes around usually comes around, and in most cases, it's going a lot faster.

I've found that the easiest way to eat crow is while it's still warm. The colder it gets, the harder it is to swallow.

For me, working out is like hitting my thumb with a hammer, it always feels so dang good when I stop. I'll never have those 6 pack abs and I've known that for over half a century. I'm okay with it.

Never could understand why some people think it's silly to wear both suspenders and a belt at the same time, you back up your computer don't you?

When you close your eyes and imagine "freedom" what comes to mind? Most people would say noble things like freedom of religion, the Bill of Rights, or the Constitution. For me it's always been the wind, nothing is as free as the wind; you never know where it came from, or where it's going.

Probably the one question you will ask most in your life, and the hardest one to get answered, at least with an answer you can accept and live with, is "why?" Sometimes, only God knows the answer.

You can never control what others do to you or say about you, but you can always control how you react.

Remember, it's not enough to learn how to ride; you also have to learn how to fall.

Good judgment comes from experience and a lotta' that comes from bad judgment.

The way you are seen by other people directly reflects on your upbringing. Never give people reason to believe you were found lying on the prairie and raised by a pack of coyotes.

Think of life as a never ending lesson, some lessons you learn easily and others the hard way. Early on I set a goal to try and learn at least one new thing every day, doesn't have to be earth shaking. Why, when, where and how are words I used often.

Live each day as though it is your last, and treat all your friends and loved ones as if it were theirs. Someday, it will be. This is a lot easier said than done, and some days I failed miserably.

When it comes to atheists, thank God they are wrong.

Tellin' someone to get lost and makin' 'em do it are two different propositions.

Try and never lose track of the people you love and care about, you may never be able to find them again and their absence leaves an awful hole in your heart.

There is nothing you could ever do, no sin big enough, to disqualify you from God's grace.

Son,

I know I've given you an awful lot of things to think about, chances are you won't remember them all, and that's okay. But the one thing I hope you never forget is how much your grandpa loves you. I have thought for many years that I was the most generously blessed man on earth, and when God blessed me with you, I was convinced. When the Lord takes me home, be strong for your grandma and every night when you go to bed, think of you and me, the fun times we had together, and smile. I'll always be up ahead, on down the road a piece waitin' for you to catch up.

Love,
Papa